Happy Birthday 'Sweet 16'

Tell her you're glad she's 'Sweet 16' with this bracelet she can wear today and spend tomorrow!

Fold Bracelet

MATERIALS: 16 new bills

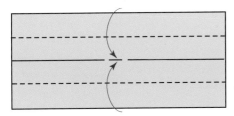

1. Fold a bill in half lengthwise, crease. Unfold. Fold the top and bottom edges to center.

4. Fold ends to the center.

2. Fold the bill in the center.

5. Fold left side over right side.

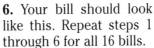

6. Your bill should look like this. Repeat steps 1 through 6 for all 16 bills.

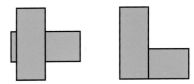

3. Fold bill in the center and unfold.

Assemble Bracelet

7. Slide one bill inside the layers of another bill to lock together forming an L.

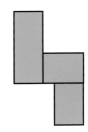

8. Slide the third bill into the second bill forming a zigzag.

9. Continue until one bill is left. Unfold the last creases in bill so it is only folded from end to end. See step 2. Slide this longer bill into the layers of the previous bill. Tuck the loose ends inside the first bill in bracelet to complete the circle.

Adorn your favorite 'royal' head with a crown fit for a king. If needed add extra bills to the bracelet to make the crown.

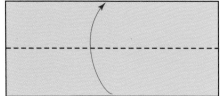
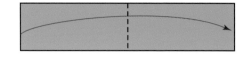
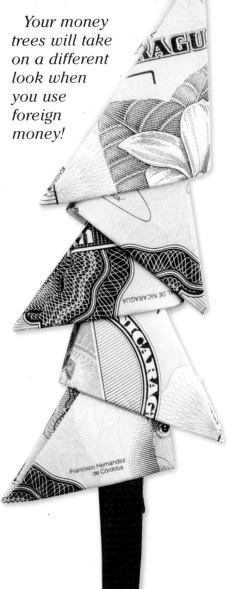

Your money trees will take on a different look when you use foreign money!

Fold Tree

MATERIALS FOR EACH TREE: 5 new bills • 2⅞" x 5⅞" piece of Brown paper • Craft stick • 2-way glue

1. Fold a bill in half and crease.

2. Fold the bill left end to match the right end.

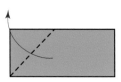

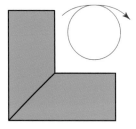

3. Fold top layer up.

4. Turn bill over. Repeat with bottom layer.

5. Your bill should look like this.

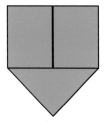

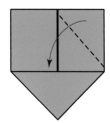

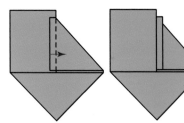

6. Open top layer like turning a page.

7. Fold right corner down. Fold end over the matching centers.

8. Turn back edge. Your bill will look like this.

Assemble Tree

1. Fold the right side to the left side. Your bill should look like the diagram.

Legs

Double Pocket

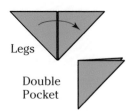

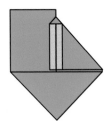

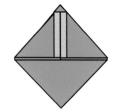

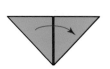

9. Open the last fold. Press down to make a triangle. Your bill should look like this.

10. Repeat steps 7-9 on the left side. Your folded bill will look like this.

11. Fold top down.

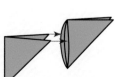

2. Insert leg of second bill into double pocket of first bill.

3. Continue inserting bills staggering the placement.

Fold Tree Trunk

Using Brown paper, repeat steps 1 through 5 for tree. Glue trunk inside the tree.

These trees grew from money and never has the forest been so green. Imagine the delight in that special person's eyes when they see your gift!

Special Occasion Cake

MATERIALS: Desired number of money trees • Small craft sticks • Decorated cake
INSTRUCTIONS: Make money trees. Insert craft stick in one fold of tree trunk. Push ends of craft picks in cake.

Tree Greeting Card

MATERIALS: Two money trees • 6" x 9¾" piece of Dark Green cardstock • 4" x 5¼" piece of Light Green cardstock • ⅝" Green letter stickers • Deckle scissors • Double-stick tape
INSTRUCTIONS: Fold Dark Green cardstock in half for card. Trim Light Green cardstock with deckle scissors and tape to center of card. Tape money tree to right side of card. Apply letter stickers.

Double Your $ TIPS

For a retirement party, use a dome-shaped cake that resembles a hill. Frost the hill with Green frosting or sprinkle with Green coconut to resemble grass. Arrange small plastic houses on hill and insert money trees.

Use plastic mortarboards for a graduation cake decorated with school colors.

Use party hats and confetti sprinkles for a bright birthday cake.

TIP

Write the message of your choice and use this card for a special occasion... birthday, graduation, retirement, baptism or just because you care!

Wonderful Hearts

Everybody loves a big heart, so… send your loved ones a special message hidden in a money heart.

Fold Hearts

MATERIALS: 1 new dollar bill

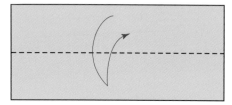

1. Fold a bill in half and crease.

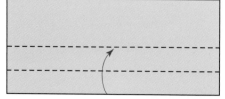

2. Fold the bottom edge to the center crease.

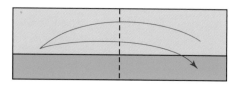

3. Fold the right side to match left side. Open fold.

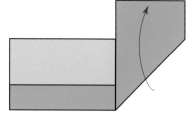

4. Fold the bottom to the center crease.

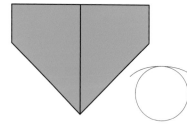

5. Repeat on the other side. Turn over.

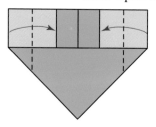

6. Fold right and left edges to meet other fold.

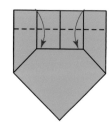

7. Fold top edges down to the center.

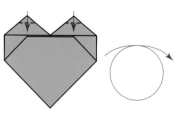

8. Fold top corners down like this.

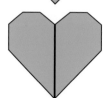

9. Fold the top points down. Turn the bill over for heart.

'Secret Message' Heart

MATERIALS: 1 new dollar bill • Computer generated message
INSTRUCTIONS: Make heart. Insert message in front fold of heart.

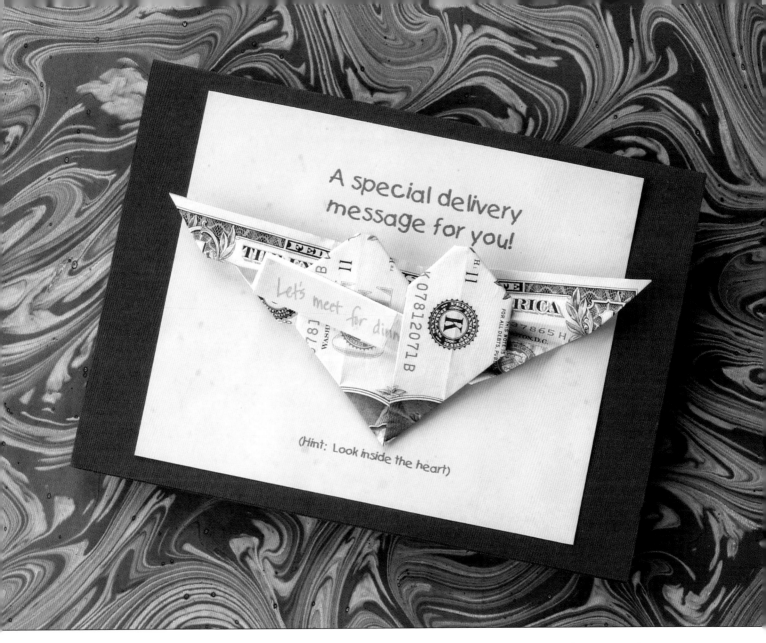

Fold Heart Wings

MATERIALS: 1 new bill

This card is so easy to make, just fold your bill following the easy step-by-step instructions, and add your computer generated message!

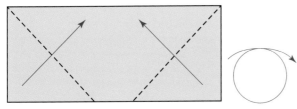

1. On back side, fold bill left and right corners to the top edge.

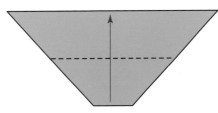

2. Turn the bill over. Fold the bottom edge to the top edge.

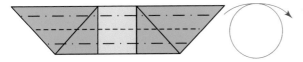

3. Fan fold by making valley fold on dashed line and mountain folds on dash-dot line.

4. Pinch the bill center and fan out wings on each side. Attach to the back of the heart.

Flying Heart Card

MATERIALS: 2 new bills • 6" x 10" piece of Burgundy cardstock • ¹⁄₂" x 5" strip and 4¹⁄₂" x 5¹⁄₂" piece of Yellow paper • Metallic Green pen • Computer generated message • Double-stick tape

INSTRUCTIONS: Fold cardstock in half for card. Print greeting on Yellow paper. Tape in center of card. Fold heart and wings. Attach to card with tape. Write message on strip of paper with pen. Insert in fold of heart.

Fluttering Butterflies

For a truly 'green' bouquet, insert folded butterflies in a live plant or add a beaded body to your butterfly for a touch of very artistic elegance.

Pot of Butterflies

MATERIALS: 6 new bills • 20 gauge wire for stems • Brown chenille stem • Potted plant • Wire cutters • Round-nose pliers
INSTRUCTIONS: Make 3 butterflies omitting antennae. Cut wires for stems to different lengths and wrap around center of butterfly. Add chenille stem antennae. Insert stems in soil.

Fold Butterflies

MATERIALS: 2 new bills

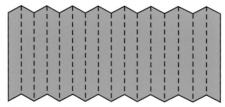

1. Make 15 fan folds in one bill.

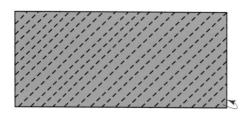

3. On second bill, fold back lower right corner ⅛". Fan fold diagonally across bill making 24 creases.

2. Crease and fold in half. Set aside.

4. Pinch the center, and fold over. Place the first folded bill under the second folded bill and secure with thin wire.

5. Wrap 20 gauge wire around center to make stem. Wrap chenille stem around center and form antennae. Fluff out wings.

Butterfly with Bead Body

MATERIALS: 2 new bills • 3" of 28 gauge wire • 20 gauge for stem • 14" of 24 gauge Green wire • Brown chenille stem • Beads (6mm x 8mm Teal oval, 7mm Bronze disk, 11mm x 34mm Teal teardrop) • Wire cutters • Round-nose pliers
INSTRUCTIONS: Make the butterfly omitting antennae. Fold Green wire in half and twist together leaving 2" straight on each end. Spiral 2" of twisted wire for end body. Insert ends of wire in teardrop, disk and oval beads. Shape antennae and cut off excess wire.

Roses, Roses Everywhere

Combine the romance of roses with the practicality of a monetary gift for an occasion that will long be remembered.

Gift Roses

MATERIALS: 10 new bills • Two 5" and four 3" pieces of 28 gauge wire • 10 stamens • Two pieces of $1/8$" dowel • Plastic corsage box • Hot Pink paper shreds • Iridescent shreds • 45" of $3/8$" Pink satin ribbon • Floral tape • Toothpick • Wire cutters

INSTRUCTIONS: Make 2 roses. Wrap dowel adding a rose and 2 leaves to each stem. Place shreds in box and add roses. Tie ribbon bow around closed box.

NOTE: To make a corsage, use 22 gauge wire for stems. Wrap stems together with floral tape and tie a bow below flowers. Insert corsage pin in stem.

Dollar Rose

MATERIALS: 5 new bills • 5" and two 3" pieces of 28 gauge wire • 3 stamens • $1/8$" dowel • Small vase • Floral tape • Toothpick • Wire cutters

INSTRUCTIONS: Make rose and 2 leaves. Attach rose to dowel with wire and wrap dowel with floral tape adding leaves as you wrap. Insert rose in vase.

TIP
Use vases of money flowers for table decorations at a wedding shower or baby shower. Then present them to the bride or mother-to-be.

Fold Leaf

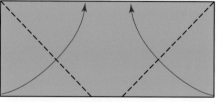

1. Fold left and right corners of bill up.

Fold Roses

MATERIALS: 3 new bills for rose • One bill for leaf • 3" and 5" of 28 gauge wire • 4 or 5 stamens • Dowel, 16 gauge wire or twig for stem • Floral tape • Toothpick • Wire cutters • 2-way glue

Note: Decide on front or back of bill. Fold all bills the same way.

1. Fold $^3/8$" ends of bill to back.

2. Fan fold center of bill and tie with 5" of wire.

3. Repeat with other 2 bills. Wire each to the previously folded bill with folded ends to back of flower. Stagger sections.

4. Curl corners of each bill to back with toothpick.

5. Cup each bill up to form flower shape. Twist wire ends of stamens together. Wrap wire to back of flower to secure stamens.

Complete Rose
  Wrap flower wire around stem. Wrap stem with floral tape adding leaves as you wrap.

TIPS
  Make a corsage for any special occasion. Moms, grandmothers and daughters will love the thought.
  Use a single rose for a boutonniere. Your favorite gentleman will be impressed.

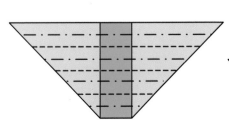

2. Make 7 fan folds across bill.

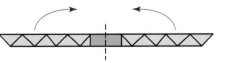

3. Fold in half.
Optional: Glue edges to secure right and left sides together.

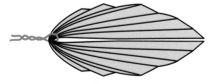

4. Insert 3" wire in fold, twist ends to secure.

Fold Pinwheel

This card spins with good wishes that you can take to the bank!

MATERIALS: 1 new bill

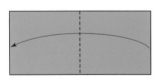

1. With front of bill facing up, fold in half from right to left.

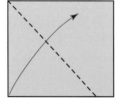

2. Fold bottom left corner up to form a triangle.

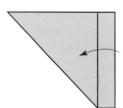

3. Fold right edge over triangle.

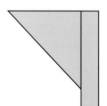

4. Your bill should look like the diagram.

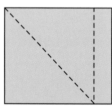

5. Unfold triangle.

6. Making sure right side stays creased, lift top layer at bottom left corner and fold to back so right fold is now inside.

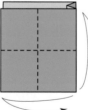

7. Make vertical and horizontal creases in bill.

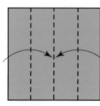

8. Fold left and right edges to center crease.

9. Fold top and bottom edges to center crease.

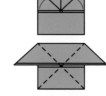

10. Pulling on the underlayer of these triangles, pull them out to the sides as far as they go to create pointed flaps. Crease.

11. Fold the left flap to point upward.

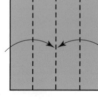

12. Rotate the paper 180 degrees and repeat steps 10-11.

Variation. Reverse fold 2 opposite flaps.

Here's a great gift or party idea - make a bouquet of pinwheels or you may prefer to add them to an existing bouquet or plant. No matter what you decide, you can't go wrong with these delightful, colorful pinwheel favors. Just follow our easy step-by-step folding instructions for this so-easy project!

Happy Birthday Bouquet Card

MATERIALS: 3 new bills • 8" x 11" piece of Yellow cardstock • 4" x 6½" piece of Yellow plaid paper • Three ½" x 4" strips of Dark Green cardstock • Computer generated greeting • Scallop scissors • Double-stick tape

INSTRUCTIONS: Print greeting on Yellow cardstock. Fold in half. Tape plaid paper to center front. Trim Green strips with scallop scissors. Make 3 pinwheels. Tape strips and pinwheels as shown.

Pinwheel Favors

MATERIALS: 3 new bills • Three 5" cocktail straws • 18" each of ⅜" mylar ribbon (Pink, Gold, Blue) • Double-stick tape

INSTRUCTIONS: Make pinwheels and tape to ends of straws. Tie ribbon under pinwheels and curl.

Simple Sandals & High $$$ Boots

A cute way to present a money gift… a pair of sandals or boots. Tuck them inside a fancy bag and your gift is ready… no wrapping required!

Fold Sandals

MATERIALS FOR EACH SANDAL: 1 new bill

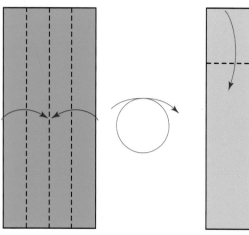

1. Fold bill in half, crease. Unfold and fold edges to the center.

2. Turn over and fold top down one fourth of the length of the bill.

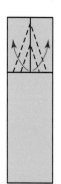

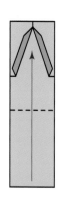

3. Make 2 diagonal folds for straps on each side.

4. Fold bottom edge up and tuck under straps.

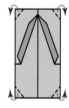

5. Fold all corners under for a rounded look.

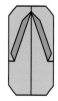

6. Your bill will look like this diagram.

Sandals Gift

MATERIALS: 2 new bills • Blue printed paper • 2-Way glue
INSTRUCTIONS: Cut small bag from Blue paper. Fold and glue bag referring to pattern. Cut two ¾" x 2" strips of paper for handles. Fold handles in half, fold right and left sides to center and glue to secure. Glue ends inside bag. Make sandals and insert in bag.

Fold Boots

MATERIALS FOR EACH BOOT: One new bill

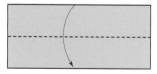

1. Fold bill in half, crease.

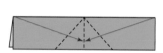

2. Make center crease. Fold top edges to center.

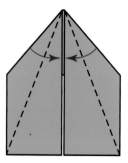

3. Fold top outside creased edge to center.

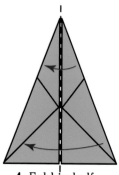

4. Fold in half.

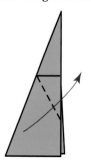

5. Fold bottom half of top layer only on the dotted line.

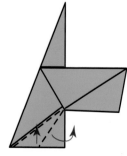

6. Fold lower right corner back and remaining section up to left.

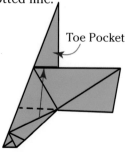

Toe Pocket

7. Fold lower section up and tuck into toe pocket.

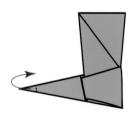

8. Mountain fold toe to remove point.

Boots Gift

MATERIALS: 2 new bills • Red printed paper • 2-Way glue
INSTRUCTIONS: Cut bag from Red paper. Fold and glue bag referring to pattern. Cut two ¾" x 2" strips of paper for handles. Fold handles in half, fold right and left side to center and glue to secure. Glue ends inside bag. Make boots and insert in bag.

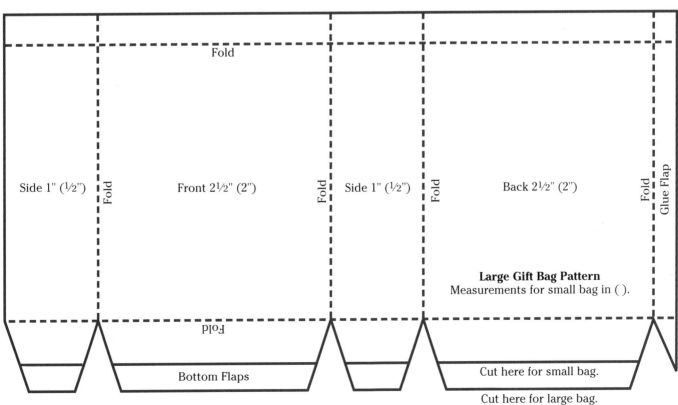

Side 1" (½")

Fold

Front 2½" (2")

Fold

Side 1" (½")

Fold

Back 2½" (2")

Fold

Glue Flap

Fold

Large Gift Bag Pattern
Measurements for small bag in ( ).

Fold

Bottom Flaps

Cut here for small bag.

Cut here for large bag.

Fold Ties

MATERIALS FOR EACH TIE:
1 new bill

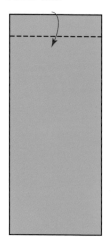

1. Fold down ⅝" at top front of bill. Make crease in the center.

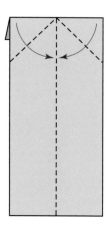

2. Turn over and fold left and right corners to center crease.

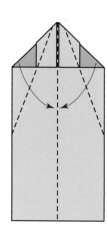

3. Fold top edges to meet in center making sure folded edges go under flap made in step 1.

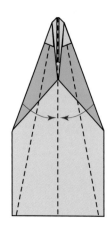

4. Repeat bringing folded edges to the center.

5. Fold the bottom corners up to make point.

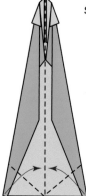

6. Fold edges of knot to match edges of tie. Fold top point down.

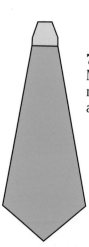

7. Turn over. Make adjustments to knot as needed.

For that 'hard to buy for' man in your life, attach a money tie to a little paper shirt… great for Father's Day and birthdays too!

Shirt Instructions

MATERIALS: 7 pieces of print paper cut to bill size • Double-stick tape

INSTRUCTIONS:

Shirt - Butt the edges of 2 pieces of paper together. Tape to secure.

Pleats - For left pleat, fold ¼" under on each long edge of a bill. Mountain fold ⅝" from right edge. Valley fold ⅜" from mountain fold. Reverse measurements for right pleat on a bill. Tape pleats to center of shirt.

Collar - Make mountain fold ⅞" from one edge of bill. Valley fold ⅝" from mountain fold. Fold each side at an angle and tape on neck of shirt with plain side of paper facing up.

Sleeves - Fold bills for sleeve following collar instructions. Tape ends to back of shirt, fold to front and fold cuffs up.

Striped Shirt

MATERIALS: 1 new foreign currency bill • 7 pieces of Green stripe paper cut to bill size • Double-stick tape

INSTRUCTIONS: Make shirt following shirt instructions. Make tie and tape under collar of shirt.

Plaid Shirt

MATERIALS: 1 new bill • 7 pieces of Pastel plaid paper cut to bill size • Double-stick tape

INSTRUCTIONS: Make shirt following shirt instructions. Make tie and tape under collar of shirt.

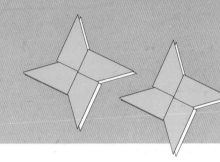
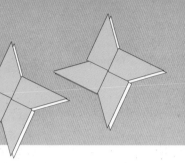

Spectacular Star Ornaments

This little money tree makes a perfect Christmas gift. Or make it in bridal shower colors for the bride and groom. You can even use the tree as a centerpiece for any of those special occasions.

Fold Star Ornament

MATERIALS FOR EACH STAR ORNAMENT: 2 new bills

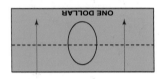

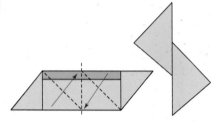

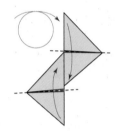

1. Place one bill upside down. Fold the bottom edge to just below the words 'One Dollar'.

2. Fold bill in half. Unfold. Fold bottom right corner to top edge and top left corner to bottom edge.

3. Fold top right edge to center. Fold bottom left edge to center. Your bill will look like this.

4. Turn over. Fold triangles at each end up. Set aside.

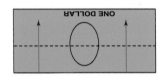

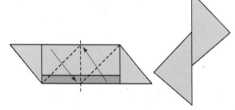

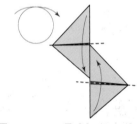

5. Place second bill upside down. Fold bottom edge to just below the words 'One Dollar'.

6. Fold in half. Unfold. Fold top right corner to bottom edge and bottom left corner to top edge.

7. Fold bottom right edge to center. Fold top left edge to center. Your bill will look like this.

8. Turn over. Fold triangles at each end up.

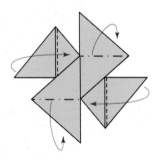

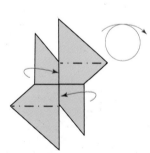

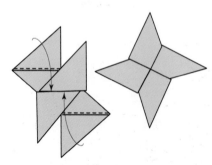

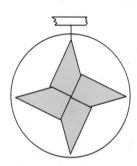

9. To join sections, place legs of one bill up and legs of second bill down. Stack bills.

10. Fold one leg down, one leg up and tuck into creased openings.

11. Turn over and repeat step 10 to complete star. Your completed star will look like this.

12. Make 9 star ornaments. Suspend stars in openings of tree with monofilament, secure with tape.

See Christmas Tree Centerpiece instructions on page 20.

Christmas Tree Centerpiece

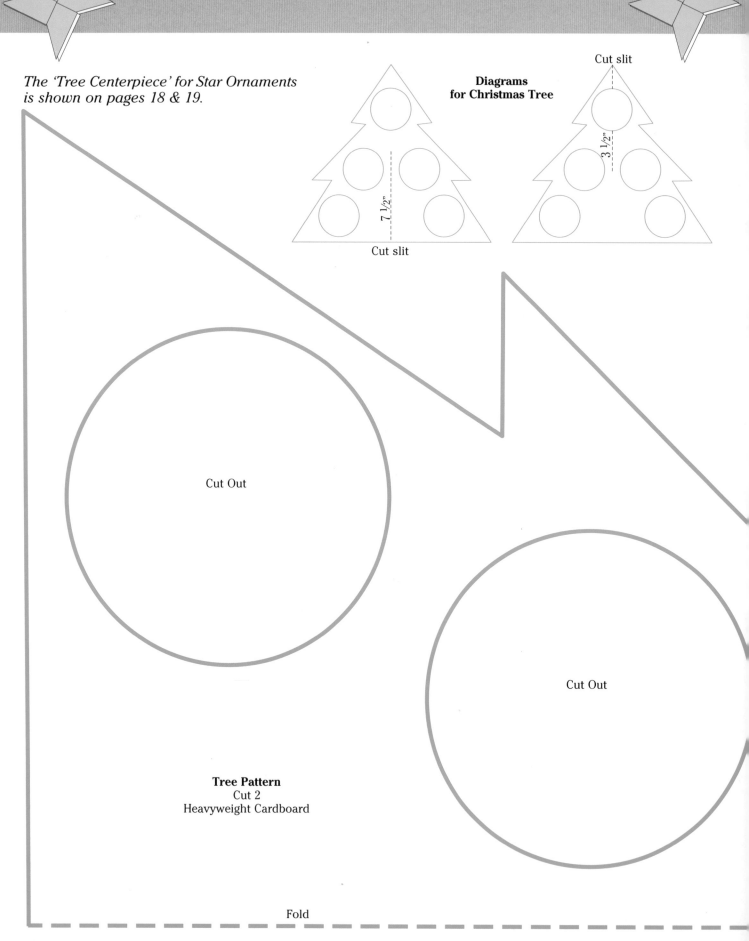

The 'Tree Centerpiece' for Star Ornaments is shown on pages 18 & 19.

Diagrams for Christmas Tree

Cut slit

7 ½"

Cut slit

Cut slit

3 ½"

Cut Out

Cut Out

Tree Pattern
Cut 2
Heavyweight Cardboard

Fold

Star & Feather Ornament

Christmas Tree Centerpiece

MATERIALS: 18 new bills • Heavyweight cardboard or foamcore • Green printed gift wrap • 3½ yards of ⅜" Metallic Gold/Silver braid • 21 acrylic stars • Monofilament • 3½" circle template • Scissors • Craft knife • Clear tape • Spray adhesive • 2-Way glue
INSTRUCTIONS: Cut 2 trees from cardboard using pattern. Spray one side of each tree with adhesive and apply gift wrap. Make sure to remove any bubbles. Cut openings and around edges leaving enough paper to fold to back. Cut slits in excess paper and glue on back of trees. Spray other side of trees with adhesive and apply gift wrap. Cut around edges and openings with craft knife. Cut slits in center of trees with craft knife. Slide tree pieces together so tree stands upright.

Make 9 star ornaments following instructions on page 18. Suspend stars in openings with monofilament, secure with tape. Tie 16 bows using 6" of braid each. Glue bows over tape on ends of monofilament and on opposite side of openings. Loop remaining braid and glue on top of tree. Glue stars in centers of bows and one star on top of loops.

Star & Feather Ornament

MATERIALS: 2 new bills • 18" of ⅜" Red satin ribbon • Red feather • Monofilament • 2-Way glue
INSTRUCTIONS: Make star ornament following instructions on page 18. Tape monofilament hanger on top of star. Glue tip of ornament to feather. Tie ribbon bow around feather and hanger.

A star ornament makes an ideal gift for your newspaper carrier, letter carrier or doorman!

Cut Out

Fold

Fold Butterfly

MATERIALS: 2 new bills • 24 gauge Purple wire • Beads (18mm x 30mm Purple teardrop, 9mm Pink disk, 9mm Yellow faceted) • Wire cutters • Round-nose pliers

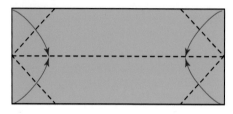

1. Fold one bill in half. Unfold. Fold corners to center crease.

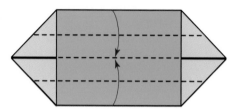

2. Fold top and bottom edges to center crease.

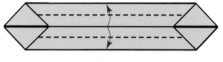

3. Fold top and bottom edges to back, Paper will look like this.

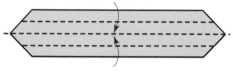

4. Turn over, bring top and bottom edges to center. Paper will look like this.

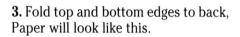
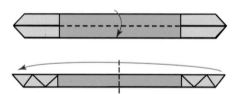

5. Fold in half. Mountain fold in half.

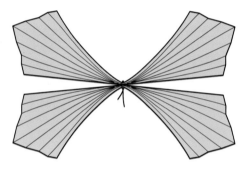

6. Open bill to resemble fan. Repeat for second bill. Attach at the center with 6" of wire. Do not cut off excess wire.

7. Cut two 12" pieces of Purple wire. Spiral 2" on one end of wires. Insert ends in teardrop, disk and faceted beads. Twist together above faceted bead to secure. Curl remaining wire around pencil for antennae. Using excess wire, attach body to butterfly below faceted bead. Wrap wire to back and cut off excess.

Make this money necklace for a wedding shower, birthday, retirement or graduation gift. The recipient will wear it with heartfelt happiness.

Money Necklace

MATERIALS: 14 new bills • 1½ yards of ⅛" ribbon • 2-Way glue • Drinking straw

INSTRUCTIONS: Make 2 hearts, 2 butter-flies, 3 rosettes and 2 half rosettes. Tape a 1" piece of drinking straw to the backs of the hearts. String all pieces together starting with the heart. Run ribbon through the straw, then through the center of the half rosette, butterfly, etc. Tie ribbon ends together.

Fold Rosette

MATERIALS: 1 new bill for half rosette and 2 new bills for rosette • Silk flower with wire stem • 2-Way glue

1. For half rosette, accor-dion fold bill 8 times. Or fan fold 16 times.

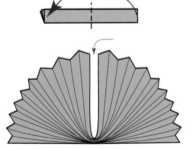

2. Fold bill in half. Glue edges together.

3. Open into fan shape. Wire wire stem of flower through fold to secure.

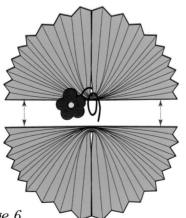

4. For rosette, make 2 half rosettes. Attach a flower to one rosette. Glue 2 half rosette edges together.

Folded Hearts shown on page 6.

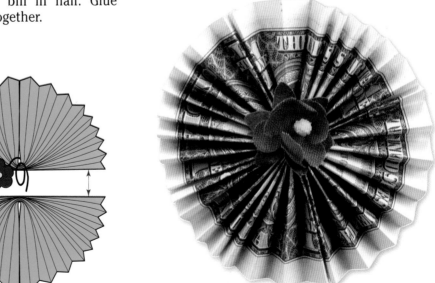

7 Bills Tux Shirt

Seven is the luckiest number ever when you present this shirt! It's sure to fit!

MATERIALS: 7 new bills • 1¾" x 6" piece of cardboard • 9" x 12" piece of White cardstock • Sheet of tissue paper • 4 Black heart pony beads • Needle and Black thread • Double-stick tape

Fold Collar

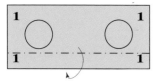 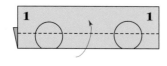

1. On back of bill, mountain fold directly above denomination number.

2. Valley fold so creased edge is right below top denomination number.

 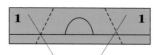

3. Turn bill over.

4. Valley fold so top corners touch.

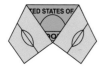

5. Collar should look like the diagram.

Fold Sleeve with Cuff

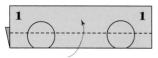 

1. Complete steps 1 and 2 for collar on 2 bills.

2. Valley fold as shown.

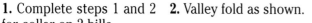

3. On both bills, valley fold top layer only being sure both numbers show.

Folded Pleats

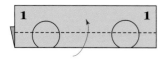 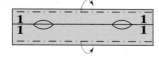

1. Complete steps 1 and 2 for collar on the 2 bills.

2. Fold borders on top and bottom to back of the bills.

Assemble Shirt

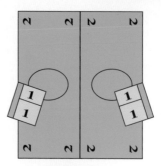

1. Place bottom edges of 2 remaining bills side by side and tape together. Tape sleeves to back of shirt, fold to front and tape to secure.

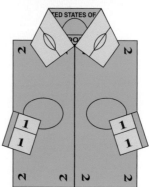

2. Tape collar to center top of shirt. Do not tape points down.

3. Sew the buttons to a piece of 1¾" x 6" cardboard equally spaced.

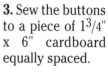

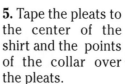

4. Butt 2 pleats on either side of buttons making sure denomination numbers are facing in opposite directions. The bills will hide the cardboard.

5. Tape the pleats to the center of the shirt and the points of the collar over the pleats.

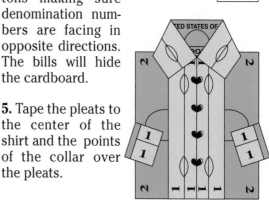

Assemble Shirt Box

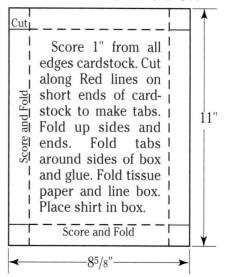

Cut

Score and Fold

Score 1" from all edges cardstock. Cut along Red lines on short ends of cardstock to make tabs. Fold up sides and ends. Fold tabs around sides of box and glue. Fold tissue paper and line box. Place shirt in box.

Score and Fold

11"

8⅝"

What a creative way to give that special man a money gift. Add a fancy tux shirt topped off with a beautiful rose for a truly spectacular presentation!

Fold Tie

MATERIALS: 1 new bill

1. Fold the bill in half, crease. Unfold and fold corners to center crease.

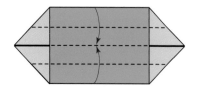

2. Fold the top and bottom edges to center.

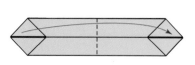

3. Fold the bill in half.

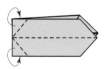

4. Make inside reverse folds.

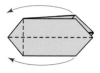

5. Fold top and bottom layers flat.

6. Fold top layer corners to the center. Turn over and repeat on the bottom layer.

7. Fold top point to the right and other point to the left.

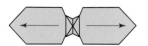

8. Pull points lightly to shape bow tie.

Tip

For really fun party wear, make a bow tie with colorful foreign currency. Pin it to the collar of your fanciest frilled shirt and have a ball!

Best Friends Memory Page

For a best friend who has 'everything', this card is a wonderful gift solution. The memory page of you and your friend is one to be cherished for years to come.

Fold Jacket

MATERIALS: 1 new bill

1. On one end, valley fold then valley fold again.

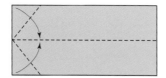

2. Turn over. Fold in half, crease. Fold top and bottom corners to crease.

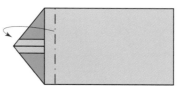

3. Mountain fold the bill on dashed line.

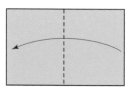

4. Fold the right edge to folded end. Turn over.

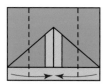

5. Fold the top layer of left and right edges to center. Squash fold upper half.

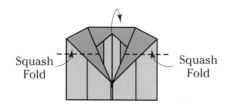

Squash Fold   Squash Fold

6. Mountain fold along the dashed line. Turn over.

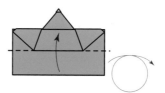

7. Valley fold bottom edge up. Turn over.

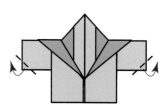

8. Fold bottom corners of sleeves back.

Fold Hat

MATERIALS: 1 new bill • 1" of paper twist

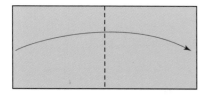

1. Fold the bill in half.

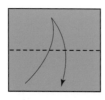

2. Crease center.

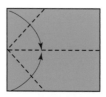

3. Fold the top and bottom corners to crease.

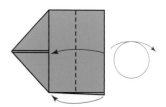

4. Valley fold edge of top layer to base of triangle. Turn over and repeat.

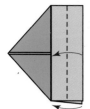

5. Valley fold edge to base of triangle. Turn over and repeat.

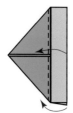

6. Valley fold top and bottom layers.

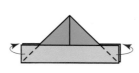

7. Turn 90°. Fold the corners against the triangle.

8. Spread the sides apart and fold small triangles to inside.

9. Finished hat should look like diagram. For tassel, cut fringe in end of paper twist and insert in fold.

& Card

'Best Friends' Scrapbook Page

MATERIALS: 4 new bills • 1" of Orange paper twist • Cardstock (9½" x 12" Dark Green, 3½" square Dark Red mat, two 5" squares Dark Red for hearts, 8½" x 11" Tan, White) • ½" and ¾" Red letter stickers • 1" circle punch • Decorative scissors • Black permanent pen • Pink chalk • Double-stick tape

INSTRUCTIONS: Trim Tan cardstock with decorative scissors. Tape to Dark Green. Cut 2 Dark Red hearts. Trim hearts with decorative scissors and draw lines with pen. Mount hearts, mat and photo. Apply stickers.

Punch circles from White cardstock. Draw faces with pen and blush cheeks with chalk.

Make 2 jackets and 2 hats. Insert tassel in one hat. Assemble friends on page referring to photo.

'Best Friends' Card

MATERIALS: 4 new bills • 1" of Orange paper twist • Cardstock (5" square Dark Red, 5" x 11" Tan, White) • ½" Green letter stickers • 1" circle punch • Decorative scissors • Black permanent pen • Pink chalk • Double-stick tape

INSTRUCTIONS: Fold Tan cardstock in half for card. Cut Dark Red heart. Trim heart with decorative scissors and draw lines with pen. Mount heart on card. Apply stickers.

Punch circles from White cardstock. Draw faces with pen and blush cheeks with chalk.

Make 2 jackets and 2 hats. Insert tassel in one hat. Assemble friends on card referring to photo.

Very Good Fortune Cookies

Fold Cookie

MATERIALS FOR EACH COOKIE: 1 new bill • ½" x 2½" printed fortune

Good fortune comes in a small package when you fill a take-out box with these unusual cookies.

1. Fold the bill on the dashed line.

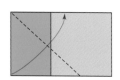

2. Fold left corner to meet top edge.

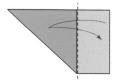

3. Fold right edge along edge of triangle. Unfold.

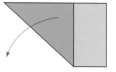

4. Unfold triangle.

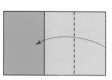

5. Refold the right side to form a square.

6. Fold corners to back. Unfold.

7. Reverse corner folds to inside.

8. Rotate so one corner is facing you. Roll the bottom corner to overlap the top corner. Tack with glue.

9. Insert fortune.

10. Insert pointer fingers in each end and bend cookie in half.

Super Surprise Box

Surprise someone you love with best wishes that spring forth from a little box.

Fold Pants

MATERIALS: 1 new bill

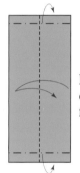

1. Fold the bill in half, unfold. Fold on dashed lines for cuffs.

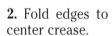

2. Fold edges to center crease.

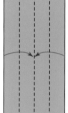

3. Fold the right edge to the left edge.

4. Fold in half.

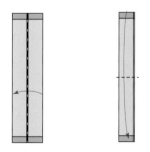

5. Your bill should look like this.

Folded Jacket shown on page 28.

Fold Box Spring

MATERIALS: Four 1" x 11" strips of paper • 2-Way glue

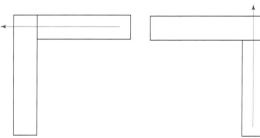

1. Overlap paper strips 1" to make two 1" x 21" strips, glue. Glue ends together as shown.

2. Alternate folding back and forth to ends of strips. Glue ends to secure.

Surprise Box

MATERIALS: 2 new bills • Four 1" x 11" strips of White paper • 7/8" doll head bead • 3" of Black chenille stem • 3" square box • Enlarged photocopy of a bill • Paper clip • 2-Way glue

INSTRUCTIONS: Trim photocopy to fit sides and top of box, glue in place. Glue paper strips together to make two 1" x 21" strips. Make spring. Glue bottom of spring in box. Make jacket following instructions on page 28. Make pants. Insert chenille stem in head and curl top. Glue stem in jacket. Insert pants in jacket, glue to secure. Attach doll to spring with paper clip. Tuck spring and doll carefully in box and close lid.

Party Favor Hats

Fold Hat

MATERIALS: 1 new bill

Make a personalized card that is also the perfect gift. Have a party at your favorite pizza parlor, letting each guest use their hat dollars to purchase game tokens.

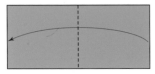

1. With front of bill facing up, fold in half from right to left.

2. Fold bottom left corner up to form a triangle.

3. Fold right edge over triangle.

4. Your bill should look like the diagram.

5. Unfold triangle.

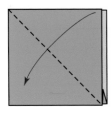  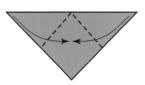  

7. With folded edge at bottom, fold upper right corner to lower left corner.

8. Turn slightly to right so bill looks like the diagram.

9. Fold right corner and left corner to bottom point.

10. Fold the top layer of lower corners up.

11. Fold upper corners out. End fold at center of square.

Party Hat Cupcakes

MATERIALS FOR EACH CUPCAKE: 1 new bill • Frosted cupcake • Plastic spoon • 12" of satin ribbon • Black permanent pen

INSTRUCTIONS: Break handle off spoon leaving 2". Draw face on spoon with pen and tie bow around handle. Make party hat and place on spoon. Insert spoon handle in cupcake.

Party Hat Place Card

MATERIALS: 1 new bill • 6" square of paper with computer generated name and greeting • Plastic spoon • 12" of 1/4" Black satin ribbon • Black permanent pen • 2-Way glue

INSTRUCTIONS: Fold paper in half for card. Break handle off spoon leaving 1½". Draw face on spoon with pen and tie bow around handle. Make party hat and place on spoon. Glue spoon on card.

Party Hat Card

MATERIALS: 1 new bill • 6½" x 8¾" piece of Dark Red cardstock • 4" x 6" piece of Tan cardstock • ¾" Red letter stickers • Plastic spoon • 12" of ⅛" Red satin ribbon • Jumbo zig zag scissors • Black permanent pen • 2-Way glue

INSTRUCTIONS: Fold Red cardstock in half for card. Trim Tan cardstock with scissors, glue on front of card. Apply letter stickers. Break off handle so spoon fits on card. Draw face with pen, tie bow around handle. Glue spoon on card. Make party hat and place on spoon. If the spoon is rough, file with emery board or nail file.

6. Making sure right side stays creased, lift top layer at bottom left corner and fold to back so right fold is now inside.

12. Fold one layer of bottom corner up.

13. Fold edge up again.

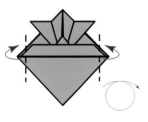

14. Fold side corners to the back.

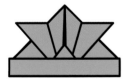

15. Turn over and fold up remaining triangle. Open the hat slightly to stand up.

Norma Eng

Norma is a native of Seattle, Washington, and has an education degree from the University of Washington. She learned Origami as a child and has taught the ancient art for more than 20 years.

Norma continues to teach Origami and is the featured instructor in an educational video series on the subject. Norma's other loves include crafts, Chinese cooking and traveling. She finds time to quilt, sew and create handmade special occasion Origami cards.

Norma resides with her husband in Texas. They have two grown children, one living in Seattle and the other in Boston.

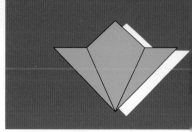

Photo corners frame a picture of the happy couple. Use this gift to buy a very special dinner!

Anniversary Card

MATERIALS: 4 new bills • Photo greeting card
INSTRUCTIONS: Make photo corners and place on card.

Leftover currency from foreign trips makes colorful photo corners for your memory album pages.

Album Page

MATERIALS: 4 new foreign currency bills • Cardstock (9½" x 12" Yellow, 8½" x 11" Dark Green, 6" x 7" Dark Red mat, 2¼" x 7" Dark Red title strip) • 5" x 5¾" piece of Yellow print paper for mat • ⅝" Black letter stickers • Corner punch • Black permanent pen • Double-stick tape
INSTRUCTIONS: Make 4 photo corners. Tape to corners of Yellow paper. Tape Dark Green cardstock, mats and photo on Yellow cardstock as shown. Punch corners on title strip, draw lines with pen and apply stickers, tape on page.

MONEY TIPS

§ Use extra large 'money' to practice folds.
§ You can also use foreign money for a different look.
§ By law, paper currency can only be photocopied in black & white, single-sided and must be reduced to 75% or enlarged to 150% of its original size.

Give a friend spending money to use on a long awaited vacation trip.

Travel Card

MATERIALS: 4 new bills • 5½" x 8" piece of Blue cardstock • 4½" x 7¼" piece of Blue stripe paper • 4" x 6" picture postcard • 'Travel' die cut • Scallop scissors • Double-stick tape
INSTRUCTIONS: Make 4 photo corners. Trim paper with scallop scissors. Tape paper and postcard on cardstock. Tape die cut at top. Tape photo corners in place.

Mount card in photo album or place in an envelope and mail to a special friend.

Suppliers - Most craft and variety stores carry an excellent assortment of supplies. If you need something special, ask your local store to contact the following companies.
Printed Paper
  Design Originals, 800-877-7820, Fort Worth, TX
Foreign Money & Extra large 'money'
  Fantastic Folds, www.fantastic-folds.com
2-Way Glue
  EK Success, Ltd., 973-458-0092, Clifton, NJ

MANY THANKS to my friends for their cheerful help and wonderful ideas!
Production Director - Kathy McMillan • Art Department Manager - Jen Tennyson
Graphic Artists - Patty Williams & Marti Wyble
Copy Editors - Wanda J. Little & Colleen Reigh • Photography - David & Donna Thomason